The Faith Of A Farmer: Daily Devotionals for Christian Farmers

Delightful Devotionals

CONTENTS

Introduction

This unique devotional journey is crafted with the diligent farmer in mind, providing daily inspiration, wisdom, and spiritual insights to accompany you throughout your agricultural endeavors. As you navigate the fields of life and cultivate the soil, let these devotionals be a source of encouragement, reflection, and connection with God.

In the world of farming, each day brings new challenges, triumphs, and opportunities for growth. This devotional aims to align these experiences with timeless biblical truths, offering a perspective that transcends the physical tasks and delves into the spiritual dimensions of a farmer's life. Whether you're sowing seeds, nurturing crops, or harvesting the fruits of your labor, these devotionals are designed to accompany your journey.

Join us in exploring the parallels between the earthly and the spiritual harvests, finding inspiration in the sacred rhythms of nature, and discovering the profound lessons hidden within the cycles of agriculture.

May this devotional series enrich your daily life, deepen your spiritual connection, and remind you that, just like a well-tended crop, your life can bear fruit that extends far beyond the visible horizon.

Day 1: Bountiful Harvest

Verse of the Day:

Psalm 67:6 (NIV) - "The land yields its harvest; God, our God, blesses us."

Reflection:

As the sun sets on the fields, casting a warm glow on the ripened crops, there's a profound sense of awe in witnessing the fruition of labor. Psalm 67:6 echoes through the rustling leaves, emphasizing that the land yields its harvest not just by chance but as a divine blessing from our Creator.

In the dance between the sower and the soil, there's a sacred partnership—a reminder that, while we toil on Earth, God's hand guides the growth. The fields become a canvas painted with strokes of providence, illustrating God's faithfulness in the cycles of life.

As you navigate the rows, contemplate the intricate connection between your work and the heavenly blessing it has on it. The bountiful harvest is a testament not only to your diligence but to the enduring promise that God blesses the work of your hands.

Journal:

1. In what ways do you perceive God's blessing in the cycle of planting, growth, and harvest?

2. Reflect on a specific harvest season. How did it strengthen your faith in God's providence?

3. Consider the parallel between the physical harvest in your fields and the spiritual harvest in your life. How can you nurture both with gratitude?

Prayer:

Heavenly Father, as I stand amidst the bountiful harvest, I'm humbled by the richness of your blessings. Open my eyes to see beyond the fields and recognize the abundance of your grace in every corner of my life. May the harvest be a constant reminder of your faithfulness, prompting gratitude to overflow from my heart. Amen.

Day 2: Seasons of Growth

Verse of the Day:

Ecclesiastes 3:1 (NIV) - "There is a time for everything, and a season for every activity under the heavens."

Reflection:

In the rhythm of a farmer's life, the changing seasons orchestrate a symphony of growth and rest. Ecclesiastes 3:1 resonates as you witness the cyclical nature of your work—each season bearing its unique tasks and lessons. The furrowed fields in winter, patiently awaiting the warmth of spring, embody the anticipation woven into the fabric of creation.

Reflect on the dance between planting and harvest, recognizing that, just as the earth cycles through seasons, so does the journey of your soul.As you plow the soil in preparation for new life, ponder the significance of your spiritual soil. What seeds have you sown in the hearts of others, and what seeds has God planted in yours?

Embrace the truth that every season serves a purpose. In moments of waiting, find solace in Ecclesiastes 3:1, knowing that God orchestrates each season, bringing forth beauty and abundance in His perfect time.

Journal:

1. Consider the current season in your fields. How does it parallel a season in your personal or spiritual life?

2. In times of waiting, what spiritual seeds has God planted in your heart? How do you nurture them?

3. How can you align your farming practices with the divine timing reflected in Ecclesiastes 3:1?

Prayer:

Gracious God, as I navigate the changing seasons on my farm, I seek wisdom to discern the seasons of my soul. Teach me patience in times of waiting and diligence in times of labor. May the rhythm of growth and rest in the fields echo the divine cadence of Your plan for my life. Amen.

Day 3: Cultivating Generosity

Verse of the Day:

2 Corinthians 9:10 (NIV) - "Now he who supplies seed to the sower and bread for food will also supply and increase your store of seed and will enlarge the harvest of your righteousness."

Reflection:

In the vast expanse of fields, there's a profound lesson in the act of sowing. As a farmer, you understand the vital role of generosity—planting seeds with the belief that they will yield a bountiful harvest. 2 Corinthians 9:10 beautifully captures the essence of this agricultural generosity, acknowledging God as the ultimate supplier of both seed and sustenance.

Reflect on your own role as a sower, not only of crops but of kindness, compassion, and love in the world. Consider the various seeds you sow in the lives of others—the encouragement shared, the support extended, and the love freely given. Just as God supplies seed to the sower, recognize the abundance of resources and blessings He has given you.

In cultivating a spirit of generosity, you participate in a divine cycle, where the harvest of righteousness multiplies. Take a moment to appreciate the interconnectedness of sowing and reaping, recognizing that your acts of generosity contribute to a harvest beyond the fields.

Journal:

1. Reflect on the ways you sow seeds of kindness and generosity in your community.

2. How has God supplied seeds of abundance in your life? In what ways can you share this abundance with others?

3. Consider the metaphorical fields of your life. What seeds are you currently sowing, and what kind of harvest do you hope to reap?

Prayer:

Almighty God, thank You for supplying the seeds of abundance in my life. Teach me to sow with a generous heart, knowing that You will enlarge the harvest of righteousness. May my actions echo Your divine generosity, creating a ripple effect of love and kindness. Amen.

Day 4: Tending to the Soil of the Heart

Verse of the Day:

Luke 8:15 (NIV) - "But the seed on good soil stands for those with a noble and good heart, who hear the word, retain it, and by persevering produce a crop."

Reflection:

In the intricate dance of farming, the quality of the soil is paramount to a successful harvest. Luke 8:15 draws a parallel between the seed on good soil and a heart that is noble and receptive to the word of God.

Reflect on your own heart as the soil of your life. Consider the ways in which you cultivate a heart that is open, noble, and receptive to the divine seed.

Take a moment to examine the soil of your heart. Are there stones of doubt that need removal, or thorns of distraction that require pruning?

Just as you tend to the physical soil, engage in practices that nurture the spiritual soil of your heart. Hear the word, retain it with mindfulness, and persevere in faith. Understand that the condition of your heart impacts the spiritual crop you produce in your life and the lives of those around you.

Journal:

1. Reflect on the state of the "soil" in your heart. What elements contribute to its richness, and what might hinder its fertility?

2. Consider the seeds of God's word that have been planted in your life. How can you actively nurture and cultivate them?

3. In what ways can you create an environment in your life that fosters the growth of a noble and good heart?

Prayer:

Heavenly Father, help me tend to the soil of my heart. Remove stones of doubt, prune thorns of distraction, and cultivate a heart that is receptive to Your word. May my life produce a bountiful spiritual crop that glorifies You. Amen.

Day 5: Seasons of Planting and Harvest

Verse of the Day:

Ecclesiastes 3:1 (NIV) - "There is a time for everything, and a season for every activity under the heavens."

Reflection:

Farming unfolds in the rhythm of seasons – from the diligent sowing of seeds to the joyous harvest. Ecclesiastes 3:1 reminds us of the divine order in the timing of each season. As you navigate the seasons of your life, reflect on the synchronicity of God's timing.

Consider the moments of planting – the times of hard work, preparation, and investment in your endeavors. Acknowledge the seasons of harvest – the moments when you reap the fruits of your labor and witness the fulfillment of God's promises.

Take a moment to recognize the current season of your life. Are you in a season of sowing, patiently planting the seeds of dreams and efforts? Or are you in a season of harvest, enjoying the fruits of your labor? Embrace the wisdom that comes from understanding the divine timing in your life. Trust that God orchestrates the seasons for a purpose and that each phase contributes to the beautiful tapestry of your journey.

Journal:

1. Reflect on the current season of your life. What are you sowing, and what are you harvesting?

2. Consider the challenges and joys of the different seasons you've experienced. How has God been present in each phase?

3. How can you align your actions with the divine timing in your life, trusting in God's plan for each season?

Prayer:

Gracious God, thank you for the divine order in the seasons of my life. Grant me wisdom to discern the timing of planting and harvest. Help me embrace each season with gratitude and trust in Your perfect plan. Amen.

Day 6: Nurturing Growth in Faith and Fields

Verse of the Day:

Mark 4:20 (NIV) - "Others, like seed sown on good soil, hear the word, accept it, and produce a crop—some thirty, some sixty, some a hundred times what was sown."

Reflection:

In the parable of the sower, Jesus illustrates the importance of fertile soil for seed growth. Similarly, the soil of our hearts and minds determines the growth of our faith and endeavors. Today, consider the quality of the soil in your life. Reflect on the receptivity of your heart to the seeds of God's Word and the dreams you plant in the fields of your work.

Take a moment to evaluate the condition of your spiritual and professional soil. Are there areas that need tending, such as removing rocks of doubt or thorns of distraction? How can you nurture the soil to ensure a bountiful harvest? As a farmer tends to the land, cultivate the spiritual and professional environments that foster growth, allowing God's Word and your efforts to flourish and bear abundant fruit.

Journal:

1. Reflect on the condition of the soil in your heart and mind. What factors contribute to its fertility or challenges?

2. Identify any "rocks" or "thorns" in your life that may hinder spiritual and professional growth. How can you address or remove them?

3. Consider practical steps to nurture the soil of your faith and fields. How can you create an environment conducive to growth?

Prayer:

Heavenly Father, cultivate the soil of my heart and endeavors. Remove any obstacles that hinder growth and allow Your Word and my efforts to flourish. May the harvest be abundant for Your glory. Amen.

Day 7: Seasons of Planting and Harvest

Verse of the Day:

Ecclesiastes 3:1 (NIV) - "There is a time for everything, and a season for every activity under the heavens."

Reflection:

In the rhythm of life, there are distinct seasons—times for planting, nurturing, and harvesting. Reflect on the current season you find yourself in. Is it a time for sowing seeds of new ideas, nurturing existing things, or reaping the rewards of your labor?

Acknowledge the divine orchestration of these seasons and trust in God's perfect timing. Just as you wait patiently for the right moment to harvest, recognize that some things in life also require time and patience.

Find contentment in the present season, knowing that God is at work, and each phase is part of His master plan.

Journal:

1. Identify the current season in your life—whether it's a season of planting, nurturing, or harvesting. How does this resonate with your spiritual journey?

2. Consider the lessons each season brings. What can you learn from the unique challenges and blessings of your current season?

3. Reflect on the concept of divine timing. In what areas of your life do you need to exercise patience and trust in God's timing?

Prayer:

Heavenly Father, guide me through the cycles of life. Help me recognize and appreciate the season I am in, trusting Your perfect timing in every aspect of my journey. Amen.

Day 8: The Fertility of Good Soil

Verse of the Day:

Matthew 13:8 (NIV) - "Still other seed fell on good soil, where it produced a crop—a hundred, sixty, or thirty times what was sown."

Reflection:

Reflect on the condition of your inner soil. Is it receptive, open, and ready to receive the seeds of wisdom, faith, and love? Like you diligently cultivate the earth, nurture the soil of your being through prayer, meditation, and reflection.

Recognize that the quality of the soil affects the growth of the seeds planted within it. As you encounter various experiences, emotions, and thoughts, be intentional about cultivating a heart and mind that are receptive to the divine seeds sown by God.

Allow the Word of God to take root, grow, and bear fruit in your life, producing an abundant harvest of virtues and spiritual richness.

Journal:

1. Assess the condition of the soil in your heart and mind. What factors contribute to its fertility, and are there any challenges you need to address?

2. Reflect on the types of seeds you are intentionally planting in your inner soil. How can you nurture a fertile ground for spiritual growth?

3. Consider the fruits you desire to see in your life. How can you align your thoughts, actions, and intentions to cultivate a bountiful harvest?

Prayer:

Gracious God, help me tend to the soil of my heart and mind. May it be fertile ground for Your Word to take root and flourish, producing a rich harvest of virtues. Amen.

Day 9: The Seasons of Patience

Verse of the day:

James 5:7 (NIV) - "Be patient, then, brothers and sisters, until the Lord's coming. See how the farmer waits for the land to yield its valuable crop, patiently waiting for the autumn and spring rains."

Reflection:

Consider the farmer's patience as they wait for the seasons to unfold. Reflect on the patience required in your own journey. In the realm of farming, there is an acknowledgment of the necessary waiting periods—the anticipation of the rain that brings life and the patience for the harvest to ripen.

Likewise, in your life, there are seasons of waiting, growth, and fruition. Embrace the lessons that each season brings, recognizing that patience is not merely the ability to wait but the attitude with which you wait.

Allow the waiting periods to be times of spiritual growth, trusting that,, your patience will be rewarded with a bountiful harvest in due time.

Journal:

1. Identify a current season of waiting in your life. How can you embrace patience and find meaning in this period?

2. Reflect on the lessons you've learned during previous seasons of waiting. How have these experiences shaped your character and faith?

3. Consider the metaphorical harvest you are awaiting. What spiritual fruits do you hope to see in your life, and how can patience contribute to their growth?

Prayer:

Heavenly Father, teach me the art of patience in the waiting. May I trust Your timing and find purpose in each season of my life. Amen.

Day 10: Nourishing Roots of Gratitude

Verse of the Day:

Psalm 28:7 (NIV) - "The Lord is my strength and my shield; my heart trusts in him, and he helps me. My heart leaps for joy, and with my song, I praise him."

Reflection:

Consider the intricate process of planting seeds, nurturing them, and witnessing the growth that follows. Reflect on the parallel in your life—the seeds of gratitude that, when planted and nurtured, grow into a harvest of joy. In the busyness of life, it's easy to overlook the small seeds of blessings.

Take a moment to cultivate gratitude in your heart. Acknowledge the sources of strength and joy, recognizing them as gifts from God.

Just as you tend to the soil in your farm, tend to the soil of your heart by nourishing it with the waters of gratitude. As you do, watch how it transforms your perspective and brings forth the fruits of joy and praise.

Journal:

1. List three things you're grateful for today. How do they contribute to your overall well-being?

2. Reflect on a challenging season in your life. Can you identify any seeds of gratitude that grew from that experience?

3. Consider someone who has been a source of strength and support. How can you express gratitude to them today?

Prayer:

Heavenly Father, thank you for the seeds of joy and strength you've planted in my life. Help me cultivate a heart of gratitude, recognizing Your hand in every blessing. Amen.

Day 11: Weathering Life's Storms

Verse of the Day:

Isaiah 25:4 (NIV) - "You have been a refuge for the poor, a refuge for the needy in their distress, a shelter from the storm and a shade from the heat."

Reflection:

Think about the resilience of a tree standing tall in the midst of a storm. It weathers the winds, bends but does not break, drawing strength from its roots. In a similar way, life brings storms—challenges and difficulties that threaten to shake us. Reflect on the source of your resilience. What roots anchor you when life's storms come?

Consider the ways God provides refuge and strength during the storms of life. Just as a tree relies on its roots for stability, you can turn to your spiritual roots for strength. Take a moment to acknowledge the storms you've faced and recognize the shelter God has provided. Your ability to weather challenges is a testament to the depth of your roots.

Journal:

1. Recall a challenging time in your life. How did you find strength and refuge in God?

2. Consider the roots of a tree as a metaphor for your faith. How can you deepen and strengthen your spiritual roots?

3. Reflect on a recent difficulty. What lessons or insights can you draw from that experience?

Prayer:

Dear Lord, thank you for being my refuge and strength in the storms of life. Help me deepen my roots in You, finding stability and resilience in your love. Amen.

Day 12: Cultivating Patience in the Harvest

Verse of the Day:

Galatians 6:9 (NIV) - "Let us not become weary in doing good, for at the proper time, we will reap a harvest if we do not give up."

Reflection:

As a farmer, you understand the importance of patience in the cycle of planting, growing, and harvesting. Reflect on the parallel in your life—times when you've sown seeds of kindness, hard work, or perseverance. Consider the waiting periods and the eventual harvest. How does patience manifest in your journey?

Think about the times impatience may have crept in, urging you to give up prematurely. The verse reminds us not to grow weary in doing good, emphasizing the promise of a harvest in due time. Contemplate the areas in your life where patience is required, and acknowledge the potential rewards of persisting in goodness.

Journal:

1. Identify a "harvest" in your life that required patience. How did waiting contribute to its value?

2. Reflect on a moment of impatience. What lessons did you learn from that experience?

3. Consider an area where you need to cultivate more patience. How can you approach it with a positive mindset?

Prayer:

Lord, teach me the art of patience in all aspects of my life. Help me trust in Your timing, knowing that a bountiful harvest awaits those who persist in doing good. Amen.

Day 13: Nurturing Seeds of Gratitude

Verse of the Day:

1 Thessalonians 5:18 (NIV) - "Give thanks in all circumstances; for this is God's will for you in Christ Jesus."

Reflection:

In the rhythm of farming, gratitude becomes a powerful seed. Reflect on the diverse circumstances—favorable and challenging—that characterize your journey as a farmer. How do you cultivate a spirit of gratitude amid the changing seasons?

Consider the moments when you've reaped a bountiful harvest and how gratitude naturally surfaced. Explore the flip side—times of scarcity or hardship—and contemplate the role gratitude played in maintaining hope and resilience. How can gratitude become a constant companion in your farming life?

Journal

1. Recall a challenging season in your farming experience. How did gratitude shape your perspective during that time?

2. Reflect on a particularly abundant harvest. How did gratitude enhance the joy of that moment?

3. Identify one aspect of your farming routine that you can approach with more intentional gratitude.

Prayer:

Gracious Father, instill in me a heart that overflows with gratitude. May I find thankfulness in the richness of harvests and the challenges of sowing. Let gratitude be a guiding force in my farming journey. Amen.

Day 14: Finding Peace in the Fields

Verse of the Day:

Philippians 4:7 (NIV) - "And the peace of God, which transcends all understanding, will guard your hearts and your minds in Christ Jesus."

Reflection:

Amidst the rustling leaves and vast fields, finding peace is a precious harvest for the soul. Reflect on the moments when you've felt an overwhelming sense of peace while tending to your crops. How does the tranquility of nature become a channel for experiencing God's peace?

Consider the challenges you encounter—unpredictable weather, pest infestations, or market uncertainties.

How can you invite God's peace into these situations? Reflect on the role of inner peace in navigating the ebb and flow of farming life.

Journal:

1. Recall a specific instance when you felt a deep sense of peace in your farm. What contributed to that feeling?

2. Think about a recent challenge in your farming journey. How might cultivating inner peace have influenced your response?

3. Identify one practice or mindset shift that can enhance peace in your daily farming routine.

Prayer:

Heavenly Father, let Your calming presence be felt in the vastness of my fields. Guard my heart and mind with the peace that surpasses understanding. In the midst of challenges, may Your peace be my anchor. Amen.

Day 15: Harvesting Gratitude

Verse of the Day:

Psalm 100:4 (NIV) - "Enter his gates with thanksgiving and his courts with praise; give thanks to him and praise his name."

Reflection:

As you stand amidst the bountiful harvest, take a moment to reflect on the journey that led to this abundance. Consider the meticulous care, hard work, and the unpredictable factors that intertwine in the growth of each crop. How does cultivating gratitude transform the way you approach your harvest?

Think about the rhythm of sowing, nurturing, and harvesting. In what ways has gratitude been a companion throughout this cycle? Reflect on the connection between a heart filled with thanksgiving and the joy of reaping the fruits of your labor.

Journal:

1. Recount a specific moment during this harvest that evoked gratitude. What was it about that moment that stood out?

2. How does expressing gratitude impact your mindset as you work the fields? Reflect on the relationship between gratitude and joy.

3. Identify three things you are thankful for in this season of harvest.

Prayer:

Gracious Father, as I gather the fruits of my labor, teach me to enter Your gates with thanksgiving. May the rhythm of gratitude accompany me through every step of this harvest season. Amen.

Day 16: Seasons of Rest

Verse of the Day:

Genesis 8:22 (NIV) - "As long as the earth endures, seedtime and harvest, cold and heat, summer and winter, day and night will never cease."

Reflection:

Amidst the changing seasons, there comes a time of rest. Reflect on the significance of this season in the agricultural cycle.

How does the idea of allowing the land to lie fallow resonate with the concept of rest in your own life?

Consider the wisdom of nature in its cycles of rest and productivity. How can you apply this principle to your own life?

In what ways do you intentionally embrace periods of rest to rejuvenate and prepare for the next season of sowing and growth?

Journal:

1. Reflect on a time in your life when rest proved essential for your overall well-being. What lessons did you learn from that experience?

2. How do you currently incorporate moments of rest into your daily or seasonal routine? Are there areas where you can improve in this aspect?

3. Consider the parallels between the rest required for a fruitful harvest and the rest needed in your personal and professional life.

Prayer:

Heavenly Father, in the rhythm of seasons, I find the beauty of rest. Teach me to embrace moments of stillness, trusting that they contribute to the abundance of life. Amen.

Day 17: The Harvest of Patience

Verse of the Day:

James 5:7 (NIV) - "Be patient, then, brothers and sisters, until the Lord's coming. See how the farmer waits for the land to yield its valuable crop, patiently waiting for the autumn and spring rains."

Reflection:

Contemplate the patience you must have as you wait for the fruition of your labor. How can you apply this principle of patient expectation to your life? In what areas do you find yourself rushing the process instead of trusting in divine timing?

Consider the analogy of the harvest in relation to the goals and dreams in your life. Reflect on the ways in which patience plays a role in achieving a bountiful harvest.

How can you cultivate patience as a virtue in your journey?

Journal:

1. Recall a situation where patience led to a more favorable outcome. How did patience impact the quality of the result?

2. Identify an area of your life where impatience has hindered progress. What steps can you take to embrace patience in that particular aspect?

3. Reflect on the concept of waiting for the right season. What signs or guidance can you look for to know when it's the right time to harvest in various areas of your life?

Prayer:

Lord, grant me the strength to cultivate patience in the fields of my life. Help me trust in Your timing, knowing that the harvest is abundant when it aligns with Your plan. Amen.

Day 18: The Soil of Gratitude

Verse of the Day:

Psalm 107:1 (NIV) - "Give thanks to the Lord, for he is good; his love endures forever."

Reflection:

Consider the role of gratitude as the fertile soil for a fruitful life.

How does expressing gratitude impact your perspective on the challenges and blessings in your life? In what ways can you nurture and enrich the soil of your heart with a thankful spirit?

Reflect on the seasons of planting and harvesting in your life.

What seeds of kindness, love, and generosity have you sown, and how have they contributed to the harvest of positive experiences? In what areas can you continue to sow seeds of goodness?

Journal:

1. Recall a moment when expressing gratitude transformed a challenging situation. How did it influence your outlook?

2. Identify three things you are thankful for in the current season of your life. How can you cultivate an ongoing attitude of gratitude?

3. Reflect on the concept of sowing and reaping in the context of your relationships. How can intentional acts of kindness contribute to a bountiful harvest of positive connections?

Prayer:

Heavenly Father, teach me the art of cultivating a heart of gratitude. May my life be a testament to Your goodness, and may I sow seeds of love and kindness to reap a harvest of joy. Amen.

Day 19: The Harvest of Kindness

Verse of the Day:

Galatians 6:9 (NIV) - "Let us not become weary in doing good, for at the proper time we will reap a harvest if we do not give up."

Reflection:

As you tend to crops, consider how your actions in life cultivate the fields of human connection. Reflect on the times you've extended kindness to others. How have those seeds of kindness grown and flourished, creating a harvest of positive influence?

Think about the challenges you've faced in sowing kindness. How has perseverance and resilience contributed to the eventual harvest of good deeds? In what ways can you continue sowing seeds of kindness even in the face of difficulties?

Journal:

1. Recall a specific instance where an act of kindness, no matter how small, made a significant impact. How did it affect the recipient and yourself?

2. Consider a time when you faced challenges in being kind. What did you learn from that experience, and how did it shape your future actions?

3. Reflect on the people in your life who have sown seeds of kindness into your journey. How can you express gratitude for their impact?

Prayer:

Heavenly Father, guide me in sowing seeds of kindness, understanding that the harvest may not always be immediate. Grant me the strength to persist in doing good, knowing that, in Your time, a bountiful harvest will be reaped. Amen.

Day 20: Seasons of the Heart

Verse of the Day:

Ecclesiastes 3:1 (NIV) - "There is a time for everything, and a season for every activity under the heavens."

Reflection:

Just as the seasons change in the natural world, our hearts also experience different seasons.

Reflect on the current season of your heart. Is it a time of growth, joy, or abundance? Or are you navigating through a season of challenge, waiting, or rest?

Consider the cycles of planting and harvest in your life. How do these cycles align with the seasons of your heart? Recognize that each season serves a purpose in the overall rhythm of life.

Embrace the lessons and opportunities that each season brings, trusting in the divine orchestration of your journey.

Journal:

1. Identify the current season of your heart. How does it correlate with the external seasons or events in your life?

2. Reflect on a past season that brought significant growth or transformation. What lessons did you learn, and how did it shape your character?

3. Consider any challenges you may be facing in your current season. How can faith and patience guide you through these times?

Prayer:

Gracious Lord, thank you for the seasons of the heart, each with its unique purpose. Grant me wisdom to navigate through the different seasons of life, trusting in Your divine timing and purpose for my journey. Amen.

Day 21: Eternal Harvest

Verse of the Day:

Galatians 6:9 (NIV) - "Let us not become weary in doing good, for at the proper time we will reap a harvest if we do not give up."

Reflection:

As you conclude this devotional journey, consider the concept of an eternal harvest. In the life of a farmer, the harvest is a time of reaping the rewards of hard work, patience, and faith. Similarly, in the spiritual realm, our efforts to sow goodness, kindness, and love contribute to an eternal harvest.

Reflect on the seeds you've planted in your life—acts of kindness, words of encouragement, and moments of love.

How do these actions contribute to an eternal harvest? Recognize that, just as you persevere through seasons as a farmer, your perseverance in doing good will also yield a lasting impact.

Journal:

1. What "seeds" have you intentionally planted in your life, relationships, and community?

2. Consider a time when you felt weary in doing good. How did you overcome that weariness, and what positive outcomes resulted from your perseverance?

3. How does the concept of an eternal harvest inspire you to continue sowing goodness in your life?

Prayer:

Heavenly Father, I thank you for the promise of an eternal harvest when we do not grow weary in doing good. Grant me strength, perseverance, and a heart that continually seeks to sow seeds of love and kindness. May my actions contribute to an everlasting harvest that glorifies Your name. Amen.

Conclusion

As we conclude this inspiring journey, I invite you to reflect on the profound connections between your daily labor and the eternal truths embedded in these pages. Your dedication to the land, the crops, and the cycles of nature mirrors the intricate dance of life orchestrated by God.

Remember, every seed sown, every crop harvested, and every challenge overcome is a testament to your resilience, faith, and the divine partnership you've cultivated. Your role as a farmer extends beyond the fields; it's a sacred stewardship entrusted to you by the Almighty.

May these devotionals continue to be a source of strength, wisdom, and inspiration as you face each day with unwavering determination. In the words of Galatians 6:9, "Let us not become weary in doing good, for at the proper time, we will reap a harvest if we do not give up." Keep sowing with purpose, tend to your fields with diligence, and trust in the promise of a bountiful harvest.

May your fields be abundant, your spirit resilient, and your journey as a farmer be filled with the grace of the divine. As you sow, so shall you reap, not just in the fields but in the abundant harvest of a life well-lived.

With warmest wishes and gratitude,

73

Delightful Devotionals

www.ingramcontent.com/pod-product-compliance
Lightning Source LLC
Chambersburg PA
CBHW061357140726
47997CB00003B/1250